NELSON MANDELA

South African President and Civil Rights Activist

by Kris Woll

Content Consultant
Dr. Marcia Chatelain
Assistant Professor, History
Georgetown University

Core Library

An Imprint of Abdo Publishing
www.abdopublishing.com

www.abdopublishing.com

Published by Abdo Publishing, a division of ABDO, PO Box 398166, Minneapolis, Minnesota 55439. Copyright © 2015 by Abdo Consulting Group, Inc. International copyrights reserved in all countries. No part of this book may be reproduced in any form without written permission from the publisher. Core Library™ is a trademark and logo of Abdo Publishing.

Printed in the United States of America, North Mankato, Minnesota
092014
012015

Cover Photo: Theana Calitz-Bilt/AP Images
Interior Photos: Theana Calitz-Bilt/AP Images, 1; David Brauchli/AP Images, 4; Rainer Lesniewski/Shutterstock Images, 7; Nic Bothma/epa/Corbis, 9; North Wind Picture Archives, 11; Jurgen Schadeberg/Getty Images, 12; Bettmann/Corbis, 16; Red Line Editorial, 18; Mary Benson/Felicity Brian Literary Agency/Sygma/Corbis, 20; Hulton-Deutsch Collection/Corbis, 24, 26; Louise Gubb/Corbis, 28, 30; Brooks Kraft/Corbis, 34; Edmond Terakopian/AP Images, 37, 45; Bryan Denton/Corbis, 39; Matt Dunham/AP Images, 40

Editor: Arnold Ringstad
Series Designer: Becky Daum

Library of Congress Control Number: 2014944216

Cataloging-in-Publication Data
Woll, Kris.
 Nelson Mandela: South African President and Civil Rights activist / Kris Woll.
   p. cm. -- (Newsmakers)
Includes bibliographical references and index.
ISBN 978-1-62403-643-9
1. Mandela, Nelson, 1918-2013--Juvenile literature. 2. Presidents--South Africa--Biography--Juvenile literature. 3. Political prisoners--South Africa--Biography--Juvenile literature. 4. Anti-apartheid activists--South Africa--Biography--Juvenile literature. 1.Title.
968.06/5092--dc23
[B]

2014944216

CONTENTS

CHAPTER ONE
The Journey Begins 4

CHAPTER TWO
Johannesburg 12

CHAPTER THREE
Prisoner #46664 20

CHAPTER FOUR
Father of a Nation 28

CHAPTER FIVE
Freedom for All 34

Important Dates 42

Stop and Think 44

Glossary 46

Learn More 47

Index 48

About the Author 48

THE JOURNEY BEGINS

On May 10, 1994, Nelson Mandela was inaugurated as the president of South Africa. The vast majority of South Africa's population was black. Yet Mandela was the first black president in the country's history. His election marked a great change. A white minority had ruled South Africa for centuries. The 1994 election was the first time many black citizens had been allowed to vote.

When he took the oath of office, Mandela made South African history.

They elected Mandela. Crowds of people gathered to celebrate the historic occasion.

Mandela sought to heal the wounds caused by discrimination. For years, inequality was everywhere in South Africa. A system called apartheid made it law. Mandela himself was just barely out of prison. He had spent 27 years there for opposing racist policies.

But on the inauguration day, the focus was on reconciliation. People looked to their remarkable new president. Mandela's journey to that stage had been long and difficult.

A Diverse Country

The history of South Africa includes the influences of many peoples. Several ethnic groups lived in the area long before Europeans arrived. People from other parts of Africa also settled there. Modern South Africa is a diverse nation. There are 11 official languages and many others are spoken informally.

Early Years

Nelson Mandela was born Rolihlahla Mandela on July 18, 1918, in the Eastern Cape region of South Africa. He was born into the Thembu tribe. The Thembu are one of the

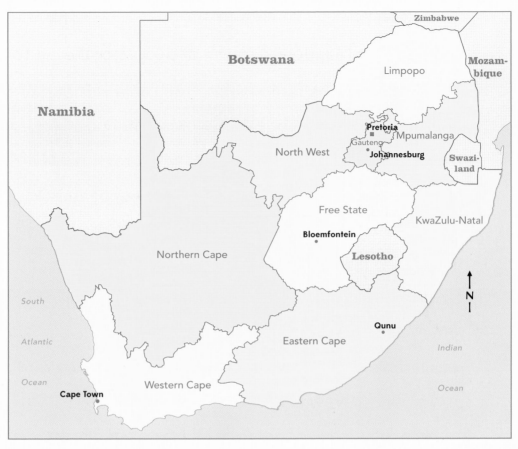

South Africa

Take a look at this map showing South Africa. Notice that Mandela's home region is not near South Africa's major cities. How do you think life was different in the rural areas?

Xhosa peoples. They had lived in that area for a very long time. *Rolihlahla* means "troublemaker" in the Xhosa language. In some ways, Rolihlahla would live up to that name.

Rolihlahla's father was an advisor to the Thembu leader, Jongintaba Dalindyebo. Rolihlahla was one of his father's 13 children. He spent his childhood in the village of Qunu. Round mud huts with grassy roofs formed the center of the village. The huts contained no furniture. The women of the village prepared meals over open fires. Most people dressed in simple blankets tied at the waist. Later in life, Rolihlahla remembered his childhood as a happy one. He recalled his village as a lovely place. "Nature was our playground," he wrote.

When he was seven, Rolihlahla started attending school. He was the first person in his family to do so. For school, he received his first pair of pants. His father cut a pair of his own pants to fit his son. The school in Qunu was a mission school. Europeans had started it to teach students about European culture. Rolihlahla's teacher called him the English name "Nelson." He went by Nelson for the rest of his life.

Rolihlahla grew up in the village of Qunu in South Africa.

Living in the Great Place

Nelson was 12 when his father died in 1930. He was sent to live with Jongintaba. He moved into the leader's home, which was known as "the Great Place." The Great Place was very different from Nelson's simple Qunu home. The tribal leader owned many luxury items, including a car.

Important meetings occurred at the leader's home. Nelson listened as people discussed politics and history. He learned things he hadn't learned at school. He learned about South Africa's dark past.

The tribal leaders taught about violent white settlers. These colonists forced tribes away from their land and traditions.

Jongintaba treated Nelson like his own son. He gave him opportunities few black South Africans could access. In 1939, Nelson started college at the University of Fort Hare.

Nelson seemed to be on his way to a life in tribal leadership. In reality, he would one day lead an entire nation. But there was still a long journey ahead.

European settlers in South Africa often forced native people to work in mines and other places.

CHAPTER TWO

JOHANNESBURG

Mandela left the University of Fort Hare after just one year. He and his good friend Oliver Tambo were expelled after protesting against school leaders. They were upset because leaders were not paying attention to student requests for better food. It was the first time Mandela stood up for a cause.

Mandela began working at a law firm in Johannesburg in the 1940s.

He did not return to Jongintaba after leaving school. While Mandela was at the university, the leader had selected a woman from the village for Mandela to marry. Arranged marriages were normal. However, Mandela did not want to get married in that way. To avoid the marriage, Mandela ran away to the large city of Johannesburg.

Johannesburg was hundreds of miles from his home. Mandela learned a great deal in the time he spent there. Some of what he learned was through school and work. Mandela finished his college degree through the University of South Africa. He found a job at a law firm and started working toward a law degree.

But much of what he learned was through experience. In the

The City of Gold

Johannesburg is the largest city in South Africa. People have lived in the area since the Stone Age. The modern city grew when gold was discovered in nearby mines in 1886. Locals call it Egoli or Jozi, and it is known as "the city of gold."

Eastern Cape, Mandela had mostly lived with other black South Africans. In Johannesburg Mandela encountered white South Africans, called Afrikaners, every day. All around him he saw racism, poverty, and segregation. Whites lived in nice neighborhoods. They had cars and paved roads. Blacks lived in areas such as Alexandra, where Mandela rented a room. Alexandra didn't have electricity or running water.

The African National Congress

Mandela reconnected with his college friend Tambo in Johannesburg. He made new friends, too. Mandela and his friends attended meetings of the African National Congress (ANC) starting in 1942. The ANC encouraged black people to create political change. To do this, they would need to gain voting rights and get access to good schools and jobs. Mandela helped start a special part of the organization focused on youth called the ANC Youth League (ANCYL). The ANCYL hoped to get students involved in politics.

Tambo remained a friend and partner to Mandela for decades.

In 1948 the National Party came to power in South Africa. The National Party was made up of Afrikaners. The National Party wanted to keep political power and resources in the hands of whites. It created apartheid, a legal system of racial segregation.

Apartheid limited the freedoms of nonwhite South Africans. There were white-only jobs, schools, and neighborhoods. Only white South Africans were allowed to vote in major elections. This ensured that leaders with other ideas could not be elected.

Members of the ANC and ANCYL, including Mandela, actively opposed apartheid. They organized nonviolent acts, such as boycotts and peaceful protests, to resist these laws. Acts of defiance spread from Johannesburg and Cape Town to smaller cities.

Arrested

In late 1955, Mandela and many other members of the ANC were arrested for opposing the government. Mandela and the others involved were put on trial but were not convicted. The government, however, kept a careful watch on the activists.

Civil Rights in the United States

People who fought against inequality in the United States also used boycotts, strikes, and peaceful protests against unjust laws. One of the biggest leaders of the US civil rights struggle was Dr. Martin Luther King, Jr. US civil rights activists paid close attention to the struggles in South Africa.

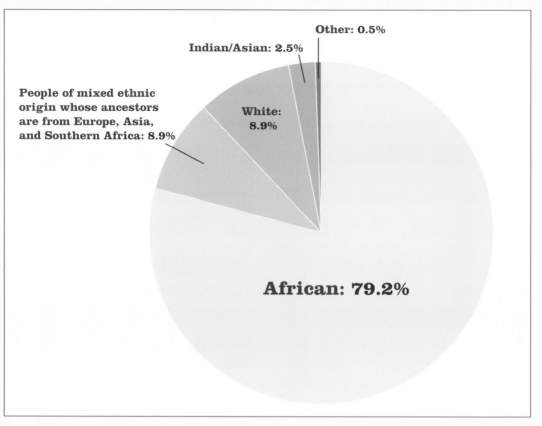

Other: 0.5%

Indian/Asian: 2.5%

People of mixed ethnic origin whose ancestors are from Europe, Asia, and Southern Africa: 8.9%

White: 8.9%

African: 79.2%

South Africa's Population

Take a look at this graph detailing the diversity of South Africa's population. While this graph is based on recent information, the country has always been a very diverse place. After reading this chapter, what surprises you about this information? Is it more diverse than you expected? Does seeing this information help you better understand Mandela's efforts and the ANC's goals?

The government did not want anyone to threaten its power.

Then, in 1960, police killed 69 people and wounded hundreds at a peaceful protest in the town of Sharpeville. Riots started all around the country. The government made membership in the ANC illegal. People were filled with fear, and Mandela grew angry. He and others decided that nonviolent protest might not be enough to end apartheid. They thought that if the government was willing to attack its own people, perhaps the people needed to fight back.

EXPLORE ONLINE

The focus in Chapter Two is Nelson Mandela's early career and activism. It also explores the history of apartheid in South Africa. The website below focuses on the history of apartheid. As you know, every source is different. How is the information given on the website different from the information in this chapter? What information is the same? How do the two sources present information differently? What can you learn from this website?

The History of Apartheid
www.mycorelibrary.com/nelson-mandela

CHAPTER THREE

PRISONER #46664

After the events in Sharpeville, Mandela continued his efforts to get rid of apartheid. He hid from the government so he wouldn't be arrested. In 1961 he became the leader of a group called Umkhonto we Sizwe, or "Spear of the Nation." The group was also known as MK. MK organized strikes and attacked government offices.

In the 1960s, Mandela's opposition to apartheid became even more intense.

In 1962 Mandela used fake documents to travel to other countries in Africa. There he met with people who were opposed to segregation. He was arrested when he returned to South Africa. Mandela was put in jail for a year.

Later that same year, the police raided an ANC headquarters in the town of Rivonia. Police arrested ANC members who they believed were plotting against the government. Mandela was linked to that plot. In October 1963, Mandela and seven others were put on trial for treason. As a part of the trial, Mandela gave a famous four-hour speech in April 1964. He explained the reasons for his actions against the government. However, his powerful speech was not enough to keep him free. He was sentenced to life in prison.

Going to Prison

Mandela was sent to the Robben Island Prison. Robben Island had been used as a prison for centuries. It was a harsh place. Mandela lived alone in a small cell without a bed. He was given little food. He had to perform hard labor. The guards abused many prisoners. Mandela's mother and one of his sons died while he was in jail. He was not allowed to go to their funerals.

After 18 years at Robben Island, Mandela was transferred to other, less harsh prisons. He continued thinking about how to create a more just world. He studied law and finished his law degree in prison. He wrote political statements that he sent to people outside of the prison. He talked about

Robben Island Prison

Robben Island Prison sits off the coast of Cape Town. It was known as a harsh place with small cells and difficult conditions. Mandela was one of many political prisoners held there. Prisoners were forced to do heavy labor in limestone quarries. They had little contact with the outside world or each other. Robben Island stopped holding political prisoners in 1991. The rest of the prison closed in 1996. It later became a museum and historic site. Former political prisoners lead tours there.

Support for Mandela grew during his decades in prison.

ways to create a peaceful, fair society. He also began writing his autobiography.

Mandela's friends and fellow activists did not forget about him. His wife at the time, Winnie Mandela, spread the word about his imprisonment. Tambo organized an effort called "Free Nelson

Mandela" in 1980. People all around the world learned about the injustices in South Africa.

As he grew older, Mandela experienced medical problems. He was sent to hospitals for treatment. Meanwhile, some members of the government tried to make deals with him. They offered him freedom if he promised to stop fighting apartheid. He did not accept their offers. He stayed in jail instead of giving up on what he knew was right.

By this time, Mandela had become known worldwide. Leaders around the world supported him. They

Mandela's Family

Nelson Mandela was married three times. He married Evelyn Mase in 1944 in Johannesburg. Evelyn was a member of the ANC. The couple had two girls and two boys. One of their daughters died from illness as a baby. They divorced in 1958. In that year, Mandela married Winnie Madikizela. They had two daughters together. They divorced after Mandela was released from prison. In 1998 Mandela married Graça Machel. He lived with Graça until his death.

Protesters encouraged people to avoid buying South African products until apartheid was ended.

argued for his release. Nations protested South Africa's policies. People stopped buying South African goods. Professors stopped working with South African universities. The country was even excluded from international sporting events. Pressure to end apartheid was increasing.

While on trial in 1964, Mandela gave a famous statement. In it, he outlined his actions and the reasons behind them:

> [The ANC's] struggle is a truly national one. It is a struggle of the African people, inspired by their own suffering and their own experience. It is a struggle for the right to live. During my lifetime I have dedicated myself to this struggle of the African people. I have fought against white domination, and I have fought against black domination. I have cherished the ideal of a democratic and free society in which all persons live together in harmony and with equal opportunities. It is an ideal which I hope to live for and to achieve. But if needs be, it is an ideal for which I am prepared to die.
>
> Source: Nelson Mandela. "I Am Prepared to Die: Statement from the Dock at the Opening of the Defense Case in the Rivonia Trial, Pretoria Supreme Court, 20 April 1964." In His Own Words. New York: Little, Brown and Co., 2003. Print. 42.

Point of View

This part of Mandela's speech outlines his ideals and how passionate he is about them. After reading it, go back and read about Mandela's antiapartheid efforts in Chapter Two. How did his point of view change between that time and the time of this speech? Why might this change have happened? Write a short essay about this shift.

CHAPTER FOUR

FATHER OF A NATION

Through the years of Mandela's imprisonment, pressure to end apartheid grew. People worked to change South Africa. Outside the country, foreign governments demanded fair laws for South Africa's people. All around the world, concerned people called for Mandela to be set free.

Then, in 1989, F. W. de Klerk was elected president of South Africa. He had been a part of the

The 1989 election of de Klerk, *left*, helped bring about the end of apartheid.

Mandela's release brought about new hope for peace and equality in South Africa.

National Party. However, de Klerk no longer believed in apartheid. He called for the end of legal racism. He also freed political prisoners, including Mandela. Mandela became a free man on February 11, 1990.

Upon his release, Mandela began working toward a new, peaceful South Africa. He preached a message of reconciliation. He also practiced forgiveness. "As I walked out the door toward the gate that would lead to my freedom," he said about the day he was released from jail, "I knew if I didn't leave my bitterness and hatred behind, I'd still be in prison."

His Long Walk to Freedom

After he was released, Nelson Mandela published his autobiography. The book is called *Long Walk to Freedom*. It tells the story of his life from his childhood to his election as president. A shorter version of the story for children was released in 2009. A movie about Mandela's life came out in 2013. Mandela wrote and contributed to other books too, including a collection of African folktales.

Mandela again became the leader of the ANC. He worked with President de Klerk and other political leaders. Together they created a government that would allow all South Africans to have a voice. Some people thought war might break out. There were a few violent incidents in 1992 and 1993. These events drove Mandela, de Klerk, and other leaders to seek peaceful solutions. In 1993, President de Klerk and Mandela were jointly awarded the Nobel Peace Prize for their efforts.

On April 27, 1994, South Africa held its first democratic elections. Finally all South Africans could vote. It was Mandela's first time casting a ballot. The ANC's party easily won the election. On May 9, the party elected Nelson Mandela president of South Africa.

The Election of 1994

The election of April 27, 1994, was historic. After three centuries, the white minority would no longer rule South Africa. It was also the first democratic election in South Africa's history. Millions of South Africans were suddenly eligible to vote. In the election, South Africans voted for political parties. The ANC won the majority of votes. The party made Mandela the new leader of a new South Africa.

In 1993, Nelson Mandela and President F. W. de Klerk were jointly awarded the Nobel Peace Prize for their efforts in creating a postapartheid South Africa. The chairman of the prize committee explained why they were selected:

> They have both chosen not to dwell on the deep wounds of the past. In so doing, they are different from leaders in many other conflict areas, even though the wounds in South Africa were deeper than perhaps anywhere else. Mandela and de Klerk have chosen reconciliation rather than the alternative, which would inevitably have been an ever more bitter and bloodier conflict. Another aspect of the policy of reconciliation is compromise and the recognition that one must give in order to be able to take. Political action on this basis reflects the highest political virtue.
>
> Source: Francis Sejersted. "Award Ceremony Speech." Nobel Peace Prize. Nobel Prize, 1993. Web. Accessed 27 May 2014.

What's the Big Idea?

Review this excerpt closely. Why were Mandela and de Klerk selected for this prestigious international award? Pick out two reasons the speaker gives for their selection. Based on this speech, what makes Mandela and de Klerk peacemakers?

FREEDOM FOR ALL

Mandela served only one term as president. Still, he accomplished many things in that time. He created a commission to heal the wounds of apartheid. He worked with other South African leaders to create new, fair laws. His government included people from diverse backgrounds. And he worked to improve the living conditions of black South Africans. He

Mandela worked together with white and black South Africans to create a more just government.

A Commission for Reconciliation

A special commission was created so that people could share their stories from apartheid and seek reconciliation. People who suffered and people who caused suffering were all invited. The commission sought to bring healing to the country. It heard testimony in special courts. It tried to foster reconciliation rather than revenge.

introduced laws to address inequality and poverty. These problems still exist in South Africa, but the country has made significant progress.

Mandela finished his term as president in 1999 at 80 years old. But he did not quit working. He continued to be a global leader. He started the Nelson Mandela Foundation to promote peace and justice. He also became involved in efforts to fight AIDS. This disease affects millions of people in South Africa. It took the life of one of his sons.

Admiring Mandela

People all around the world admired Mandela's work. In 2008 a huge crowd celebrated his ninetieth

Many celebrities and musicians paid tribute to Mandela on his 90th birthday.

birthday in London, England. Crowds cheered as he took the stage. "Where there is poverty and sickness, including AIDS, where human beings are being oppressed, there is more work to be done," Mandela told the crowd. "Our work is for freedom for all."

Mandela's last public appearance came during the 2010 World Cup. The tournament was held in

South Africa. Mandela was a lifelong soccer fan. He was thrilled for his nation to host people from around the world. His appearance at the closing ceremony was widely reported. He gave a wide smile and an excited wave to the packed stadium.

Mandela's Legacy

Mandela died on December 5, 2013, at the age of 95. He was mourned around the globe. He was buried outside of Qunu, the village of his childhood. His legacy lives on.

"I would like to be remembered not as anyone unique or special, but as part of a great team in this country that has struggled for many years, for

A diverse group of South Africans watched as Mandela's casket was brought to Qunu, the village he lived in as a child.

"THE STRUGGLE IS M
NELSON MANDE

GAOLED 5th AUGUST 19
SENTENCED TO LIFE IMPRISO
12th JUNE 1964 FOR HIS ACT
AGAINST APARTHEID

ERECTED BY THE GREATER LONDON COU
UNVEILED BY OLIVER TAMBO
PRESIDENT OF THE AFRICAN NATIONAL CONG
28th OCTOBER 1985

NELSON MANDELA WAS RELEASED
AFTER 27 YEARS' IMPRISONMENT
11th FEBRUARY 1990

RDED THE NOBE

Statues and other memorials like this one in the United Kingdom have been built around the world to remember Mandela's life.

decades and even centuries," Mandela said in his appearance at the World Cup. "The greatest glory of living lies not in never falling, but in rising every time you fall." Mandela rose each time he fell along his journey. And along the way, he helped lift up others.

FURTHER EVIDENCE

Remembering Nelson Mandela

There is a lot of information about Mandela's achievements in Chapter Five. Chapter Five also talks about Mandela's legacy. What is one of the main points of this chapter? What key evidence supports this point? Go to the below website about Mandela's life. Find a quote from this website that supports the chapter's main point. Does the quote support information already given in this chapter? Or does it add new information to it?

The Life of Nelson Mandela

www.mycorelibrary.com/nelson-mandela

IMPORTANT DATES

1918

Rolihlahla Mandela is born on July 18 in the Eastern Cape province of South Africa.

1930

Mandela's father dies, and young Mandela is sent to live with the Thembu tribal leader.

1942

Mandela, now living and working in Johannesburg, begins to attend ANC meetings.

1990

Mandela is released from prison.

1993

Mandela and President F. W. de Klerk are awarded the Nobel Peace Prize.

1994

Mandela votes for the first time in South Africa's first democratic election and is elected president of South Africa.

1955

Mandela and other ANC members are arrested.

1960

The Sharpeville Massacre occurs in South Africa.

1964

Mandela is convicted of treason in the Rivonia Trial and is sentenced to life in prison.

1999

Mandela ends his term as president but continues to work on important issues.

2010

Mandela appears at the World Cup in South Africa.

2013

Nelson Mandela dies on December 5.

Dig Deeper

After reading this book, what questions do you still have about Nelson Mandela and the fight against apartheid? Write down one or two questions that can guide you in doing research. With an adult's help, find a few reliable sources that can help answer your questions. Write a few sentences about how you did your research and what you learned from it.

Another View

This book has a lot of information about the history of South Africa and Mandela's leadership there. As you know, every source is different. Ask a librarian or another adult to help you find another source about South African history. Write a short essay comparing and contrasting the new source's point of view with that of this book's author. What is the point of view of each author? How are they similar and why? How are they different and why?

Why Do I Care?

How do you think Mandela's messages of fairness and equality affected the world beyond South Africa? In what ways do you think he changed people's lives, even those that were not from his country? How might the world be different without Mandela's leadership?

Say What?

Studying history and politics can mean learning a lot of new vocabulary. Find five words in this book that you've never heard before. Use a dictionary to find out what they mean. Then write the meanings in your own words, and use each word in a new sentence.

GLOSSARY

activist
a person who takes action for a political purpose

apartheid
laws enforcing segregation in South Africa

autobiography
a book written by a person about his or her own life

colonialism
when an outside country controls the people, land, resources, and government of another country

democratic
having to do with social equality and the principles of elected representation in government

minority
a group of people that make up the smaller part of a larger group

mission
a group sent to parts of the world to spread information about religion

reconciliation
reestablishing friendly relations after a period of disagreement and separation

segregation
the separation of people based on color, ethnicity, or other factors

treason
the crime of working against one's own government

LEARN MORE

Books

Kramer, Ann. *Nelson Mandela: The Rebel Who Led His Nation to Freedom.* Washington, DC: National Geographic, 2005.

Mandela, Nelson. *Nelson Mandela's Favorite African Folktales.* New York: W. W. Norton, 2004.

Pollack, Pam. *Who Was Nelson Mandela?* New York: Grosset & Dunlap, 2013.

Websites

To learn more about Newsmakers, visit **booklinks.abdopublishing.com**. These links are routinely monitored and updated to provide the most current information available.

Visit **www.mycorelibrary.com** for free additional tools for teachers and students.

INDEX

African National
  Congress, 15, 17, 19,
  22, 25, 27, 31–32
Afrikaners, 15–16
AIDS, 36–37
apartheid, 6, 16–17, 19,
  21, 25–27, 29–30, 33,
  35–36
arrests, 17, 22

colonialism, 10

death, 38
de Klerk, F. W., 29–33

Eastern Cape, 6–7, 15
education, 8–10, 13–14,
  23
election, 5, 32

family, 8–9, 25, 36

Johannesburg, 7, 14–15,
  17, 25

legacy, 38, 41

National Party, 16, 30
Nobel Peace Prize,
  32–33

presidency, 35–36

Qunu, 7–9, 38

release from prison,
  30–31
Robben Island Prison,
  22–23

Sharpeville, 19, 21
South Africa, 5–7, 10,
  18, 29, 38
support, 25–26

Tambo, Oliver, 13, 15,
  24
Thembu tribe, 6–8
trial, 22, 27

University of Fort Hare,
  10, 13

ABOUT THE AUTHOR

Kris Woll is a writer and editor. She has an MA in history and lives with her family in Minneapolis, Minnesota.